AIMING

HIGHER

Helping Employees
BELIEVE, BELONG & MATTER
in Your Organization

A Framework for Communicators

MICHAEL GREEN

Aiming Higher

Helping Employees Believe, Belong & Matter in Your Organization

A Framework for Communicators

Michael Green

Published by

Inflection Strategies

Portland, Oregon

First published January 13, 2018
Revised and updated January 23, 2018

Copyright © 2018 Michael Green

ISBN: 0999738305
ISBN-13: 978-0999738306

For Helen

CONTENTS

Part 1

Getting to 'Believe, Belong, Matter'

1
INTRODUCTION

I wasn't expecting to care so much.

When I got the call from Intel's head of HR, asking me to come help with employee communications during the major corporate restructuring that was under way, I had been with the company for 11 years, working in external communications roles. I had spent my time representing Intel's interests to the outside world of media and analysts. I was used to taking on the persona of my employer—I was used to advocating for the company's strategies, technologies and products—but it was always to those external audiences.

I knew I took on a kind of parental sense of responsibility toward the teams of people I'd led (sometimes, I'm sure, annoyingly so to those who worked for me).

But I'd never given a thought to the mindset of the entire employee population of Intel; I'd never thought about the state of "health" of the tens of thousands of Intel employees around the world; never thought about what they felt about the company, worried about, dreamt of, wanted.

I thought it was simply another *communications* assignment, with a specific audience: employees. I never expected how important those employees, those humans, would become to me, and how differently I'd come to see the "communications" assignment.

That assignment, as director of worldwide Employee Communications for Intel, consumed my work life from 2006 to 2011. One question drove me: What does every employee need to thrive? My best answer: She wants to *believe* in the organization's purpose, *belong* to a team of people helping one another soar, and *matter* to the organization and its success. I was convinced that communications could play an outsize role in creating and fostering that environment of "believe, belong, and matter."

During that 2006-2011 period, my team and I used this framework of "believe/belong/matter" to focus our programs and messaging and to remind ourselves of what was most important, to our employees and to our work.

With this book, I offer the "believe/belong/matter" framework as a way of looking at the opportunity—the *obligation*—to help employees thrive in organizations of any kind, of any size. And I challenges communicators of all types, from executives and managers to communications professionals, from business group leaders to HR practitioners, to step up.

A few notes on this book

The framework or lens of "believe, belong, matter" is the dominant theme of this book but it's not the only one. I'll share other observations and learnings from my communications work, all intended to help you get clearer faster, get more out of your efforts, and increase (or maintain) your sanity in the process.

I'll also draw from more than my work in employee communications. With decades of experience in all forms of business communications, from media and analyst relations to employee communications, I'll try to help you make the most of the communications opportunities you face—because there are *always* opportunities. I've held many different leadership roles in companies big and small, including two decades with Intel. Sometimes I've gotten it very right—and sometimes less so. Those learnings, I hope, will benefit you.

So the chapters that follow will range from dirt-simple suggestions to help you "get a project out the door" to broader explorations about how you can best help your employees thrive. Some chapters are quick-hit suggestions, some are longer essays. They reflect my belief that great messaging is worthless without disciplined delivery, that big ideas get executed with small steps. If I succeed, you'll feel helped in all of those extremes.

You'll also sense that caring for employees is at the center of everything. But caring and earnestness are not enough, and they're certainly not strategies. They need to be channeled into real-world communications aligned with business goals and organizational cultures—even if you're trying to change a culture.

Like all human efforts, this book will continue to be a work in progress. I'm continually learning from colleagues and clients, and always looking for new insights and examples. I'll share them in future editions of this book and on my blog. Your criticisms and suggestions are always welcome. Write me at mike@michaelgreencommunications.com.

2
THE LEADERSHIP AND COMMUNICATIONS OBLIGATION

It's an obligation and an opportunity for every leader: helping people believe, belong and matter in your organization.

If you're a communications professional in any company, organization or team, you this responsibility in important ways.

I mean helping your people:

- *Believe* in the purpose of the organization.
- Feel that they *belong* to a mutually supportive team.
- Trust that they *matter* in two ways: they are essential to the team's success, and they are valued by the leaders of the organization.

This isn't about happy talk or misty-eyed hugs. Those are fast ways to lose credibility and exhaust your teams emotionally.

It is about describing your honorable purpose (or developing one first if needed). Reminding everyone, regularly, that we thrive best if we support one another to thrive together. And making clear what every person's contribution is (and can become), and demonstrating that the humans making those contributions are appreciated and supported.

Like the wise woman said, this is simple but it's not easy.

This obligation and this opportunity are most in the hands of the leaders of the organization. But I offer this book to communications professionals instead, because they have a better chance of avoiding distractions (of various stakeholders); because they can elevate a willing leader's impact; and because they have the chance to touch and inform everything a company says to and does with its people.

Communications pros can also help prevent situations where it seems like a company is saying things *about* its people and doing things *to* its people that will erode an environment of believe, belong and matter.

3
WHAT TO ACTUALLY DO?

How do you implement the "believe, belong, matter" framework in your organization? What do you actually do?

Whether you're a leader, a manager, or a communications professional, the most important action is to begin thinking in terms of believe, belong and matter.

When we're regularly asking ourselves, "How can I help our employees believe, belong and matter?" our answers give us all kinds of guidance about decision, action, message and tone. This framework can inform not only communications planning but our policy formation and our business decisions as well.

For example, if the company is about to enter a new market segment to pursue more growth, create a new product line, or purchase another company, the leaders and communicators should ask themselves:

- Will this move be easy or hard to understand in terms of our goals?
- Are we asking employees to do new things, or simply to direct current skills in new directions?
- Will this step make employees instinctively more proud of the company, or less proud?
- After the transition, will the organization be even more like it is today, or different?
- Is the company making this move from strength, or to protect against a current weakness?

- Are leaders and managers prepared to help every single employee understand how her role will help the new approach succeed?

Each of your answers will affect how your employees—your human colleagues—will believe in the organization's purpose, feel they belong to a mutually supportive community, and matter to the organization in two ways: their contributions are essential to the company's success, and the company cares about their well-being.

The answers don't have to be happy ones. Life and work are full of difficult decisions with tough actions that aren't comfortable. The "believe, belong, matter" framework isn't about happy talk or false paradises. It's about recognizing that organizational strength and business momentum depend on employees who understand and commit to the company's goals, trust their leaders and colleagues, and feel like their contribution makes a difference.

It just so happens that such employees are, well, happier.

But if you're a communications adviser presenting a plan leveraging the "believe, belong, matter" framework, you can leave out the "happier" part—and just know it'll be one of the built-in payoffs.

Back to this chapter's key question: What to actually do?

Consider everything

In everything you communicate, from the CEO's strategy presentation to the vacation policies to the fire drills and cleaning schedules, think about "believe, belong and matter." Use it as a filter, a lens. Watch for opportunities to reinforce the environment in positive ways. Watch for disconnects that risk negative effects.

This framing doesn't have to take you much time. Then you can decide where upside opportunities or downside risks warrant more time—for greater clarity, for addressing natural questions, or for reconsidering the policy or business step itself.

It's complex—but full of opportunity

Understand that "belief" isn't only about business strategy, "belong" isn't just about trust and familiarity, and "matter" isn't just about job role and benefits. To believe in a company I also have to feel it treats employees fairly. To feel I belong here, I have to believe in the company's strategy. To matter, I have to trust my manager as she guides and recognizes my work.

All of these cross-influences make things more complex, but they also increase the number of opportunities for positive momentum.

Partner well

Appreciate the limits of communications—and become close partners with human resource professionals and business leaders. Each on her own can do a lot, but not nearly as much as you can do together.

And the most important aspirations—the higher aims of "believe, belong and matter"—can't be reached without coordinated and mutually supportive efforts to plan, to execute, to measure, to adjust, and to plan and execute again and again.

To be a great partner means to listen closely, to support fully, and to request support clearly. It also means (in this context) not being preachy and absolute about "believe, belong, matter." The last thing an HR pro needs is to be told by a communicator that "your policy is hurting my 'matter' goal."

But talking through the framework, pointing out the ways in which your communications work fell short of your own goals, seeking to understand the HR partner's own goals, and exploring ways that your communications work can help them—these are powerful steps toward strong and beneficial partnering.

Don't talk about it—live it

In my experience, talking publicly about "believe, belong and matter" isn't a good idea, just as declaring that you're a trustworthy person doesn't inspire confidence. It's better if the "believe, belong, matter" framework is kept inside the communications and leadership teams, as the framing for other action and communication.

It's not that they need to be secret. They're not embarrassing or strategy-sensitive.

It's just that without the right context they sound hollow. Or like someone protesting too much.

In addition, the phrase can feel preachy or misty-eyed. "So you're trying to make me a true believer?" an employee might ask in an open forum. And I'd have no trouble answering: "Not at all. I want to make sure we're pursuing and explaining strategies that you can believe in." But it would be an unnecessary distraction.

Much better if those employees simply benefit from actions and words that truly foster an environment of "believe, belong and matter."

Allocate the different strengths of leaders

Complexity, as I mentioned above, can be our friend. Just as there are multi-dimensional relationships between "believe, belong, and matter" and the stuff of work life (business strategy, HR policies, organizational culture), there are many opportunities offered by the differing strengths of executives and leaders in your organization.

Some executives and managers are terrific presenters and speech-makers on a big stage. Some are much more effective in small groups where quiet dialogue happens.

They also have different experiences and stories, and stories—examples—are your friend.

Make good use of those diverse strengths and stories. Build matrices (on whiteboards or in your head) of how those human leaders can best connect with your human employees in various settings, situations, timings, and communication modes. Invite leaders into your thinking, and leverage their suggestions. Wherever they are suggesting they help, they are likely to be energetic helpers in your mission.

In the meantime you'll be giving your employees the kind of diverse messages that will build strong foundations of believe, belong and matter.

Leverage everything

You have the sense by now that the "believe, belong, matter" framework is much more about the spirit of things than about strict DOs and DON'Ts of communications and leadership. You're right.

There are many philosophies of leadership, many modes of communications excellence. I believe every practice can benefit from the lens of "believe, belong and matter."

Many books and seminars by professionals, scientists, researchers and authors of all kinds have offered frameworks, blueprints, practices and disciplines that may resonate with you and help propel your momentum. Training and development models, the organizational application of scientific research in physiology, psychology and neurology, the intersections of societal changes and business strategies—all offer riches to be harvested.

Use them all. I don't intend to displace them. I don't pretend to have those experts' skill, experience, education or training. (See "partnering" section above.")

I do offer the "believe, belong, matter" framework as an approach that can help focus and fuel any other approach to employee strength in organizations of any kind and size.

It's a wonderful opportunity—and a serious obligation. Why attempt any less?

4
MEASUREMENT AND PROOF? NO.

Is using a "believe, belong, matter" framework a guaranteed path to strong employees? Can it be directly measured or proved?

No and no.

While the health of an organization can be measured and tracked effectively—some of my favorite people are expert at this research—I don't believe a framework such as this can be *proven* to work.

We can, of course, find correlations. I do think an organization will be stronger when its communicators and leaders have a mindset of "believe, belong and matter." I think that measurements of an organization's health (sometimes called "engagement") will be higher.

But the complexity of organizations and measurement approaches, and the varied ways that an organization could implement "believe, belong and matter," tells me that trying to directly prove a connection is a waste of precious time.

Instead, I invite you to try it on, and see if the tenor of your organization doesn't feel different.

5

WHAT ELSE WE CAN GET
FROM 'BELIEVE, BELONG, MATTER'

I think an organization operating with a "believe, belong, and matter" mindset gets some broad benefits that go by many names.

For example, you might say, in human and organizational terms, that it delivers freedom, safety, and connection.

Freedom is friction-free work. It is labor spared unnecessary bureaucracy but given the right amount of intelligent process to prevent re-work. It's disciplined, and it's respectful of others' time and my own. It comes with enough distraction-free blocks to allow focus and follow-through, and it's executed with the intelligence, experience and commitment to achieve mastery.

Safety is knowing we can make mistakes so we can keep stretching, risking and aiming for everything that's truly possible. It's feeling confident enough to constructively challenge a colleague's thinking without fear of payback. It also means not worrying about whether I can feed my family and send my kids to school. Safety is enhanced when we act like enlightened owners in our daily work decisions—helping ensure the organization's sustainable strength, and with it the jobs that address our basic needs and the careers that enable our highest ambitions.

Connection is the community and teamwork that provide the mutual support we all need to keep the dark times from devouring us and to fuel enough bright times to thrive. It's the collaboration that helps us become one huge multipart brain that multiplies our own intelligence—especially to solve the increasingly complex challenges the world now brings, whether we're competing for money or trying to ease people's burdens. It's the cooperation that builds mutual trust. It's knowing not only that we can ask for help when we need it but that our colleagues will start with "yes"—and mean it. It's keeping our egos sufficiently in check to readily acknowledge my colleagues' contributions. To be quick to say "good idea" and slow to claim "I thought of that too" (even if you did). To remember that giving others credit is a self-sustaining use of a renewable resource.

When we pursue "believe, belong, matter," these are the conditions we're aiming to create for ourselves, or share with our colleagues, and ensure for our employees. They define how a healthy organization must evolve to thrive in this increasingly complex world: aggressively reducing bureaucracy, vigorously encouraging open and direct exchange of ideas and feedback, and recognizing performance on collective as much as individual results.

In their most basic form, these three ingredients—freedom, safety, and connection—are the necessary components of good human and organizational performance. In their most elevated forms they are what make possible the kinds of lives we hope for everyone and the kinds of remarkable work we aspire to do, generation after generation.

And I think they result from the dedicated pursuit of "believe, belong, and matter."

6
AVOIDING TEMPTATIONS

With the aspirational goal of using communications to foster "believe, belong and matter," it's tempting to over-reach—to begin to think that communications can fully inspire a workforce, and to believe that an inspired energized workforce will do great things. Of course, communications can't do it by itself. As Andy Grove once said to me, "good products help."

But it's just as dangerous to conclude that communications can't do much. Those "good products" or great products come from energized teams led by honest, direct, energized leaders who benefit from their own (and their organization's) honest, direct, inspired communications.

This sounds like philosophy, you might say.

Yes, you're right. When you look at organizational communications as I do, it amounts to existential awareness, first principles, and the foundations of humanity. Too much? Maybe, maybe not....

There can be a difference between how you *look* at our communications practice and how you *talk* about it. One CEO I worked with gave me some gentle and important pushback when I was recommending a certain message, which was getting misty-eyed. "One or two mentions of 'the stakes being high' go a long way," he told me. Another time he said, "That's not us." He was right—I was taking the tone and content of our message way too far to be credible, to be helpful.

But that prudence in output doesn't mean we need to be dry in our aspirations—or in recognizing our obligations and opportunities.

Part 2

Essays on Organizational Communications (and a few other topics related to the communicator's challenge)

7
THE OPPORTUNITIES IN EVERY CHANGE

Transitions—good ones or bad ones—tell us things we didn't know before, such as what's working and what's not. They also force us to change some things, whether in location or relationships or flow. That combination is powerful. Because when we know more than we did before, and we're moving in some way, we have the chance to adjust our direction (to change where we're going) or our speed (to get there when we want).

And that's the case whether we've invited the transition or it's been, um, invited upon us.

Nothing's more important here than clarity, whether the transitions involve one person or an organization of thousands. Clarity of self-knowledge, clarity of goals, clarity of plan, clarity of commitment. If we kid ourselves about anything, our actions will be untrusted and ineffective. We won't trust ourselves, or our teams won't trust us. Nothing will happen that we want to happen, or if it does it won't last.

Listening, then, is far more important than talking. Asking questions of ourselves and others; listening with open minds and total focus; asking more questions built upon the first answers. This is the work that will help us decide what to say—to ourselves or our organizations.

And then…more listening.

8
USE BARBELLS TO CLARIFY PLANNING

The beginning of any planning cycle—whether January 1 or any day you declare a beginning—offers sense of potential, and if we're smart we'll grab that offer with both hands. Never decline an invitation to see fresh possibilities.

With us humans, though, fresh possibilities can become brown bananas. I've been thinking about an approach to capturing and keeping that sense of potential in our professional and personal planning. It uses barbells.

Stick with me for a moment.

Our smartest colleagues have done their advance planning long ago; they already knew the best time to plant an oak tree. But let's embrace the second-best time—today—and sit down with our favorite computing device or simply pen and paper.

For me, there's the rub. My own list making—er, I mean strategic planning—usually begins as an outpoured mixture of hopes and fears, guilt and grandeur, seemingly dictated by a chattering monkey for whom no hyperthought is unworthy of being recorded. (It's interesting but not helpful that this list looks like a vitamixture of strengths, weaknesses, opportunities and threats from a traditional SWOT analysis.)

Eventually the discipline of selection and execution takes hold, and my plans take shape. I apply the important filter of deciding what not to do, identifying what Peter Drucker called the "posteriorities."

But until then it's a dizzying spectacle: every chore, responsibility, and dream that could be imagined.

Such an exercise has its benefits, in exorcizing anxieties and in creating a cosmic inventory. But it sure feels like a long walk. Could we reduce time to clarity?

Answer "A," of course, is "yes." (Remember, today is a new day—the new day, actually.)

The core problem with the first draft of the list is about time; the unspoken questions are simply "what could I do?" and "what should I do?" without any timing guidance.

And if we apply the traditional timing of "near term," "mid-term" and "long-term," we still invite long-form chaos because that "mid-term" box becomes huge, filled with things we know are too difficult to do right now but that we're not willing to put off for "long."

Here's where the barbells come in. The barbell metaphor refers to two extreme opposites with nothing in between, such as an investment strategy that includes only super-safe and super-risky bets. Let's give our planning process similar extremes, and ask just two questions:

- What is the best use of my time right at this moment?
- What do I want to accomplish before I die?

When we reduce the questions to just these two, something interesting happens: they're easier to answer.

This doesn't make the tasks themselves any easier. It's still no fun to clean the bathroom or do this month's billings. It's still painful to stop procrastinating that professional project that scares you. It's still a big leap to call the parent/child/sibling you're estranged from.

26

But the items on the list are clearer—and fewer.

The mid-term actions needed in your actual plan will make themselves known later: the new options created by the "right this minute" actions and the pre-work needed for the "before I die" goals.

For now, though, there are just those two sets of answers. The list has gone from being incomprehensible to simply hard. With a built-in invitation to begin.

And what a gift that is, to ourselves or to our teams. What a powerful gift that is.

9
THE HIDDEN POWER OF YEAR-END MESSAGES

At the end of any year, when leaders are pondering (or should be pondering) their year-end messages to their teams, let's not miss an opportunity: the deep potential and power that's waiting to be harnessed in those communications.

It's easy (and no crime) to quickly write a brief note of thanks and email it out to the organization. But a great year-end communication can give an organization exactly what it needs—whether that's a big thank-you for the year behind or an urgent energy-boost for the year ahead; whether it's aligning to a new direction or reinforcing the current path with new insights.

(This applies whether you're sending an email, posting a video, or standing on stage. It applies whether you're reaching a hundred thousand employees or a half dozen.)

While delivering on the immediate need or opportunity, the strongest messages can also provide context to help employees better understand (and remember) the group's priorities. How do goals 1, 2 and 3 fuel one another? How will Team A help Team B deliver more than either team ever dreamed? What was your biggest worry in the year behind and your greatest hope for the year ahead—and what can those insights teach us? What did Susan or Bob in customer support do last year (with little fanfare) that opened up a surprising new market for us in the year ahead?

There's sometimes a stretch goal, too: to use the year-end (or new-year) message to establish a stronger messaging foundation—a powerful new story—that leaders can reinforce through the entire year ahead.

Whether you lead a global organization or manage a small team, consider the hidden power of your year-end message. Consider what your employees most need from you right now, or what you're most asking of them in the year ahead. (For bonus insights, ask yourself what message you want to be able to write a year from now.) Then make the most of this year-end message. You'll focus and energize your teams, remind them why all the hard work is worth it, and strengthen your business momentum.

10
WHAT PAUL OTELLINI TAUGHT ME ABOUT BLUSTER

When I learned of former Intel CEO Paul Otellini's death, it wasn't the big things about Paul that flashed through my mind— not his ushering in of the Wi-Fi era with Centrino laptop chips in 2003, not the massive restructuring of Intel he drove in 2006, not the surprising decision he made to retire in 2013.

Instead, it was a relatively small thing that, to me, said so much about Paul—and about Intel, the company he loved and served since he finished college. It also reminded me of what a serious leader says and does—some contrasting consolation in our current political era of hollow bluster.

That small thing was a simple remark Paul made to me in 2006, during the big restructuring, when I was running employee communications for the company.

In that role I didn't report directly to Paul (my boss, the head of HR, did). But because of the size of the restructuring and Paul's sensitivity to its impact on employees—thousands of employees leaving the company, major changes in executive roles, and large shifts in product priorities—my internal communications role meant I got to work more closely with Paul than I would have otherwise.

It seemed to me, then and now, that Paul sweated every detail of the restructuring, every change employees faced, every worry they might have about the company and its future.

With a change that big, and a leader that thoughtful, it's tempting for a communications adviser to let a tone of high drama start to infuse the memos and presentations you're drafting for the CEO. And that's exactly what I was starting to do. Paul's mantra during that time was "change before you're forced to," and in my effort to convey that message to employees I began to unintentionally inflate the story. In essence, I was taking a serious matter and enlarging it into something of cosmic proportion.

(This is another disease that we communications professionals are susceptible to—the "this is the most important moment in history!" fallacy.)

Paul recognized the slope I was slipping down. In one memo review he did some subtle nudging. "One or two mentions of 'the stakes are high' will go a long way," he told me in an email. Still, my drafts kept showing that I wasn't getting his point.

Finally, in one hallway meeting, he pointed to the draft memo in his hand, looked me in the eye, and gently said: "This isn't Intel. This isn't us."

And I got it. Our restructuring was a serious matter, but not a cosmic one. The future of the company, and the fate of tens of thousands of employees, offered more than enough weight to get our attention, without my inflating things into existential scale. The details Paul was sweating—of revenue streams and cost structures and employee rosters—would provide all the threats and opportunities needed to help us take things seriously. No additional gilding would be required.

In this way Paul was channeling the spirit of one of his CEO predecessors, Andy Grove, whom Paul once served as technical assistant (in essence, chief of staff) during his remarkable Intel career progression. Andy had little patience with what he called "misty-eyed" posturing; he just wanted leaders like Paul to aim high and then guide employees through the painstaking steps to reach those heights.

And Paul did just that for Intel. To me he was always professional and respectful, frequently funny, and often appreciative, especially as, later, I got better at drafting memos that reflected his quiet seriousness. Along the way, he always knew who he was and who Intel was—and what he helped Intel become with his intelligence, grace, and patience as he taught so many of us how to be better at our own jobs.

11
DON'T BE BORING

What do you want to say?

Confusion brings pain. I know, as one who has spent a lot of time confused.

I've learned that confusion is sometimes invited. That clarity can be a choice. A decision. A way to help you get stronger as a communicator.

In many ways, life and work and love are all about communications, because, internal or external, that's where people come to life and where people go to live. It's also where I've spent 40 years of my professional life.

Listen. We all have said to ourselves, "There must be a better way to say that." The sentiment—frustrating, hopeful, hopeless, and did I say frustrating?—afflicts us all. There are ways to get through it—none magical, none full of alchemy, no tricks to make it easy. But it can be easier. That was my goal when I was writing this for my children. Well, OK, my dream was to make it easy for them, to remove fear and pain from their lives. Then I thought: Listen. Quick. Do you really think that's possible? Would you really want to do that if you could?

There's no growth without pain to work through, not as a moral badge of honor, but simply as a fact of life—muscles and exercise and experience. But although pain is unavoidable, there's no sin in trying to forego avoidable pain. It's the avoidable pain that I hope to prevent. And it's the big bonus that comes with the opposite of confusion—clarity—that I want to help deliver.

When we're clear, we save time, we express more of what we want, we increase the chances of getting what we want, and of getting to where we want to be, whether that's an easier path or a harder path than many of our friends and family.

One tool of clarity that I've found useful for breaking through the fog is the admonition, Don't Be Boring! Years ago I would have sneered at such advice as shallow and hollow and commercial. But I've come to see it differently: humans need energy to live. We need some source of joy, of jolt. We need to understand what we care about. We need to remember what we care about. We need our loved ones to remember what we offer them.

To live with such energy means we need to have the courage to defy convention at times, or at least to not be twisted up in grief as we worry about what others think of us. As we work through all of those narratives, including the goal to be of interest to our own selves, we need to remind ourselves to be free to be odd or offensive or disappointing to others.

One great path to that is the reminder, Don't Be Boring!— because it incents and incites us to have an edge. It also reminds us that we don't need to be invisible, to "leave no trace" of our presence in the room—as if we were backpacking in the remote backcountry of a national park. I may not need to be remembered after I die. But to be invisible in the room I'm in right now, with colleagues and partners? It's not useful as a communications professional (even though our role in execution is often, appropriately, a "background" one).

Invisibility is the opposite of clarity. So Don't Be Boring!— especially to yourself.

12
IT'S NOT ABOUT WILL

We all know what to do in our communications work (or in our life). The goals, objectives, key results, messages, tasks. Why don't we do it?

It's boring to report that humans have been asking that question for millennia, when they bother to ask it at all. Maybe it's the boring-ness of doing what we know we need to do, maybe boredom is one of the greatest sources of human pain, or at least the most insidious, the one that sneaks up on us, the one that's present before we even dive into the pool.

A shrink once told me, when I was struggling with how to do all the tasks facing me, from work to parenting to marriage, and straining, straining to get it all done and get it all done right, that the answer wasn't in will—*but in planning.*

I'm comforted somewhat by the story that Einstein would carry a small notebook and pen with him when sailing. At least it tells me that his thought experiments couldn't all be worked out in his head. For me, I can barely think without writing down what I'm thinking.

The connection between clarity of thought and clarity of writing has many parts:

- Writing what you think
- Testing what you've written
- Strengthening what you've written by changing from passive to active voice, using verbs of action instead of

nouns of description, and removing all unnecessary words. Then you'll have the clear thought that represents you. It may suck but it's yours.

Then we can ask ourselves, what to do about it? Or as Roberto Unger suggests, "What should we do next?"

One of the most powerful phrases in thinking is "for example." It forces clarity from the foggiest of notions. Can you give me an example (of that most stupid notion)? you might ask yourself.

The armed forces have a practice they call "After Action Reports," or AAR, which are rundowns of what happened and how things turned out after a battle or other event. Their goal is to learn from it: what does this experience give us, and how can we take from it and apply to the next one (or to our children, we might say). It's a great habit to foster. And one of the best ways to use this is to pretend it's happened already—kind of a game-playing scenario of "what if," not too different from writing your own obituary. Let's call it a pre-mortem, or Pre-After-Action-Report, or PAAR.

Planning can be short. If you work in the technology industry you know that, almost by dictate if not by custom, it seems that no serious plan can be written in anything but PowerPoint, and no PowerPoint plan can contain anything fewer than 50 slides. It doesn't have to be thus. The legends of businesses being sketched out on cocktail napkins is real; the scarcity of space forces clarity, and the unwelcoming surface of the napkin to most writing tools (in addition to the fact that the napkins are often wet and disintegrating) forces you to get to the point quickly.

The lesson extends to any plan we're writing: we don't have to expand the plan to fill the available space of a computer's hard drive. We can choose to take a cocktail napkin approach to the most profound personal plan. Three bullets are all you need. In fact, by keeping to three bullets you do greater justice to the most profound plan, because you've pre-eliminated all the blather that would only disrespect the sacred subject, whether it's your child's education or your own cosmic future.

The value of such simple planning is at least twofold: it guides the future action, but most important, it clarifies your thought.

The sister of planning is sequencing and scheduling: what step comes before what other step, and when should step 1 occur? This (as my family can tell you) is where I fail most and biggest. I'll spare you the dime-store psychologizing and self-flagellating about why doing this is such as source of pain to me (pre-living the next day that I'm afraid of?). Let me just tell you that when my wife has forced me to sit down and put real letters and words on a calendar, with threat of either rejection or worse, the gift has been beyond enormous. Freeing. Clarifying. (It's one of the paradoxes of this book: I write it not as a consummate thinker/planner/writer, but as a struggling one.)

One of the unintended gifts of the marketing age to personal development is, I believe, this: if you're boring, nobody will notice you. If they won't' notice you, they won't listen to you. If they don't listen, they won't hear. You know what? It applies to self-talk, too. The Calvinist principles that our Catholic parents inadvertently fostered in us in our 1950s and 60s childhood may be nearer to god in their humility but they don't do much for inspiration.

So what does "don't be boring" actually give us in the way of guidance in our planning? It tells us to push to the edges and beyond—for greater clarity through extremes. This doesn't mean we have to follow through on our plans to wear a bozo-the-clown costume while bungee-jumping in Mexico with only one leg attached to the safety cord. But the process of thinking (and talking with ourselves) in the extremes is wonderfully clarifying.

We can always dial back a wild plan to something that won't kill us. But if we haven't thought of the wildest notion, how much more likely that we might miss something interesting?

This again is one area where I write from the knowledge of stumbling rather than the record of success. I'm learning, late in life, that edginess and some risk has a lot going for it in those relationships that I've been only protective of. Crisp planning with a "don't be boring" mantra is sound advice for more than one venue. And for all you tuna-casserole-weaned white guys like me: this isn't about needing to have Nijinsky-like creativity. Anyone can systematically ask where the extremes are, and then move closer to them. You'll be amazed at what it sparks.

13
THE QUEST FOR CLARITY

This chapter is about writing—sort of.

Now, there are countless books about writing, from the high-quality-density classic *The Elements of Style* to Zinsser's thoughtful *On Writing Well* to the visually descriptive handbook for students, *Writing Inc.* (They're great.)

Why would we need more words on writing?

Because there are missing connections.

This is a book about organizations and the power of a "believe, belong, matter" mindset. In a sense, it's a book about energy and passion and clarity. It aims to help in ways both small and large, from how to greet the store clerk to the choices we make about how to live our lives.

If it helps you, it will help in at least some ways at each end of that spectrum. And I'd rather it helped you in only one way at each end, than help you in dozens of ways at only one end.

Why? Because the full power of passion and commitment and clarity comes from seeing the connections between the small and the large, the everyday and the once-in-a-lifetime.

Once you begin looking at what keeps things from being clear, the list gets very long very fast.

- Our thinking isn't clear
- I'm not sure which word to use
- I don't know what I really want

- I'm afraid to expose my true thoughts because I don't want them criticized
- I haven't invested the time needed to think, or express, this clearly
- I don't want to know what I think
- I don't want to take the time to rewrite my words
- I'm afraid of what I think
- I don't appreciate the payoffs of clarity, in my thinking or in my words
- I don't want to risk failure of my clear action, of the action it's clear I need to take

This chapter might just as well have been titled "For Example" because there's nothing that can't be made clearer with examples. In fact, if you can create three examples for something, you're way ahead of the average ordinary thought.

Life and people are messy, beautiful things. They're not always inherently clear, and they can't always be made clear in the sense of simple and known. Part of our job in driving for clarity is to accept that we won't always get there, and recognize when we're not going to get there. Accepting that frustration, and living with that ambiguity, lets us not waste energy that we could put to better use in situations where we can and we must get to clarity. (Yes, it is a bit like the Serenity prayer: knowing when to drive for clarity, when not to, having the courage to drive, and the perspective to know the difference.)

Yet one good way to test the potential for clarity is to do the "three examples" test: Ask of a situation, Can I express this in three concrete examples? If the answer is truly "no," we can ask "why not?" and learn something useful about the ambiguous situation we find ourselves in.

There is no new science in this book. There is, I hope, new thinking. The "believe, belong, matter" framework and the "for example" habit are about using some creative connections about our words and our thoughts and our intentions and our actions, toward more joy and less pain. It borrows energetically from others' work and, I hope, connects things in new ways.

14
THE CLARITY OF BEING BUTTONED UP

Years ago a technology exec I worked with (who became a friend) offered advice that has stayed with me for decades. It amounts to: "Be buttoned-up."

We'd just finished a media tour, with long days and nights and no sleep, and I asked him for some feedback on how things had gone.

"I would have liked you to be more buttoned-up," he said.

"What's that mean?" I asked.

He replied: "Be crisper in your message, clearer in our goals, and more direct about what you want me to do."

The insight that keeps returning is this: when we're advising distracted people (whether they're high-powered executives or fame-hungry celebrities or attention-challenged children), we need to make sure our communication to them is super-crisp and clear, and direct enough for them to get the gist easily, make a decision confidently, or comply readily.

That's not easy and it takes time. Being brief takes longer than writing long. Getting clear ourselves about the most important point of context, or about the real action or decision needed, takes time and thought. I'm sometimes not sure what I think until I have to explain it to somebody else.

This applies to both written and spoken communication. And it isn't about fancy writing or speaking, but about clear thinking, careful selection, and good planning. It's also not about "pleasing" our audience; being buttoned up gives our recommendations a better chance of getting to "yes."

By the way, these principles can apply to all of our communications, whether to execs or peers or subordinates or children. But we owe others the effort, not because of hierarchy or obligation but because of pragmatics: they have many other things on their radar besides whatever we're addressing together. We want to make it easy for them to make well-informed and confident decisions where we're involved. And that can't happen if they aren't quite clear about our point or our request, or if they're frustrated or surprised or distracted.

There's one other aspect that is sometimes hard to define: we need to be serious-of-purpose in our guidance and recommendations to others. This doesn't always mean formal but it sometimes means "not too informal." Our message can be non-formal in the way that modern culture invites. But if it appears too casual or dashed-off, then the message can feel unworthy of the precious minutes or longer that our audience or customers need to digest it.

Now, all of this would be easy if our goals were simple, but most multi-person efforts are complicated. So are the other projects or tasks or dreams they're engaged with. Time is a finite resource. So it's our responsibility to be:

- Clear
- Direct
- Brief
- Serious of purpose

If there's really a TON of stuff to share, which this "clear/direct/brief" message doesn't encompass, then it's our job to decide what's in the summary. We can always provide more background or backup content, for details or logic, where it will help. But we need to think of that as "optional" content, and not depend on it for our message's understanding. Sometimes our audience or customer will want to dig into the background to gain more context. Sometimes they'll just be reassured by its presence even if they don't read it.

Such clarity also demands good planning so that we don't surprise anyone. Nobody wants to be rushed or surprised. It's our job to avoid those feelings. If we want our offers (plans or requests or teaching) to be digestible, we want to make sure we don't boost stomach acid.

The world gets ever more complex. Being buttoned-up will be essential.

15
DONALD TRUMP'S REAL COMMUNICATIONS PROBLEM

When Donald Trump rotated through his first press secretary, Sean Spicer, and then the communications director Anthony Scaramucci, the president no doubt had high hopes for a new morning in America, where he finally would get the media coverage he deserves.

But he kept running up against two laws of communications physics.

Because while the science and art communications are complex (since it's all about human beings), in everyday practice there are only two things that communications can do for any leader or organization.

One, communications can amplify who you are and what you're doing.

Two, communications can help you define and become who you aspire to be.

This is bad news for Trump. He doesn't actually want anyone to see who he really is and what he's really doing. And he doesn't aspire to become someone better than who he is now.

Watching the White House press team (past and present) contort themselves and their language to explain the unexplainable, I've been reminded of the communications principle that "good policies make good PR." You can't talk your way into a good reputation. It's a lesson all communications professionals learn (often the hard way), whether we're working in government, corporate or nonprofit organizations.

Consider the nicknames for the "comms" person responsible for "telling the story" of the leader or organization: megaphone, spin doctor, flack. They're usually pejorative, the label applied in either frustration or mockery.

These labels are just softer forms of "liar." Sometimes we communications professionals have earned the label. At those times, we're doing professionally what most of us do as humans: trying to appear better than we are, to get more support or less criticism than we deserve.

What we learn from experience is that communications efforts never succeed in re-directing or masking. Communications mostly exposes what's actually there—the first law of communications physics.

But the pain of that realization can present a rich opportunity. Strong communications pros ask themselves, What would our story be if we became who we aspire to be? This is how a communications team can inform not only the strategy of the leader but their moral compass—the second law of communications physics.

Here is where communications professionals earn their keep: by articulating what's possible, and then suggesting the actions (and words) to move the administration, in this case, from here to there.

There are real-world and real-human limitations to this approach, of course: the character of the leader, and the presence (or lack) of aspiration to something larger or nobler.

Each time the Trump team refreshes its press team (Sarah Huckabee Sanders now, someone else later), trust will matter—

but not for the reasons you'd first imagine. A trustworthy press secretary is a good thing for a president not because reporters will necessarily believe her. It's because reporters will listen to a trusted spokesperson for a few minutes longer than otherwise before they decide. They'll allow a moment to hear the substance of the position.

But there's the rub—substance. Trump's press secretaries will always be working from deep in the hole their boss has dug. The goal of each new spokesperson cannot be to "generate good press," because the President won't have earned that. Their first goal instead must be establishing enough trust to be listened to.

But that will require acknowledging the ludicrousness of some past positions. And what are the odds that the big boss would sit still for such an honorable and reasonable gesture?

Trump's critics have often invoked crisis comparisons to describe what they might do to repair things. Unfortunately for the Trump team, their problem doesn't have the clear margins of a crisis. The well-known crisis-management advice of speed, truth and honor applies to Tylenol (cyanide poisoning) and Intel (Pentium flaw). But for those companies there was, as they say, some there there.

So what should the next Sarah Huckabee Sanders do? Let's pretend we wanted to help Trump, and look at two options: the aspirational and the less aspirational.

The aspirational would be a path of transformation—if not toward honor, then to redemption or at least to honesty. Not very likely.

The less aspirational (and only slightly more likely) scenario says that the Trump team will either come clean about their agendas (tax cuts and de-regulation at any cost) or say, "We now realize this isn't working; here's our starting offer to Republications and Democrats to do something good for the country together."

Alas for this president, even the less aspirational path is way out of reach—because of who he is and what he wants. Donald Trump's real communications problem is that the two laws of communications physics means he will continue to get exactly the media coverage he deserves.

16
ANYTHING BUT NONCHALANCE

Quick. When did you last feel most alive?

My bet: You were lost into something or someone because you put yourself there totally.

This isn't a new idea. It's offered, directly or indirectly, by wisdom literature thousands of years old and by last week's self-help titles (and their parodies) about zones and peak experiences. But whatever we feel about ancient wisdom or current wit, there's an essential lesson here and we ignore it at our peril: We'll be dead a long time.

It sounds simple—put yourself there totally—but not so clear or easy. What to do?

I've got a suggestion, based on decades of professional, family and married life, years of thinking about this and watching the results at work and at home, and my own struggles (and failures) to live this rule.

It's this: forbid the opposite. I may not be able to always succeed in putting myself there totally. But I can try to keep myself from ever shrugging my shoulders and saying "whatever"—adopting that comfortable but unsound position of safety from self-embarrassment or hurt feelings.

The worst failing, I've learned, is nonchalance. When a friend needs a hand or a voice, when my spouse needs my soul, when my child needs my guidance, when my job needs my performance—do I hold nothing back, or do I retain a little bit for safety, to protect myself? After all, if I don't give everything, then I always have an out: I could have succeeded if I really tried, and my failure is explainable. Right?

This book is about how the "believe, belong, matter" framework can help fuel organizations. But in many ways it's about how to avoid that hazard of nonchalance, or dig out of it if we find ourselves there. It's built on what I've learned and how I've gained from the simple (but not easy) application of passion and commitment, and the magic of the joy that follows—no matter how flawed my effort. Nonchalance may not be visibly present, but it hovers everywhere—just as its antidote is always at hand if we're willing to risk it.

Once we get good at avoiding the mistake of nonchalance or indifference, our game and life can rise to another level, where we're applying so much passion and commitment that there's no room for nonchalance.

Children show us the opposite of nonchalance all the time. When my younger son was 5 or 6, on a family car trip, we approached a toll booth. He must have seen these before, because I remember him asking—urging—that he be the one to drop the money into the basket as we passed through. So when we stopped at the booth, we let him unbuckle his seat belt, and he proceeded to step up on the rear seat, reach up behind me to take the coins, and then stretch, stretch himself over my seat to lean out the window and drop the coins in the toll basket.

To this day I remember the joy he felt at this maneuver—a physically challenging, momentary burst of effort in a new activity, with no apparent payoff for him beyond the immediate stretch.

It struck me then, and I've remembered since, that this is the path to centeredness, to feeling strong: a focused application of energy and reach to get something done, and especially rewarding if it's new.

This was the path to secular salvation.

And it was anything but nonchalance.

At the opposite end of the life-work spectrum I can tell you that what makes my easygoing self get angry at the office is not so much ugly politics (because they look exactly like what they are), but rather the subtle nonchalance that people often adopt when they decide something is silly or not worthwhile. I'd rather have the ugly politics—at least they're motivated by something. But the nonchalant "whatever"—that's deadly.

We spend our precious days working, caring for loved ones, sometimes barely slogging through, sometimes striving to be better and perform better and love better. Sometimes we feel lifted by the possibilities in life; sometimes it's all we can do to bear the gravities of existence.

And if you're anything like me, you watch and listen for clues— clues to finding a shorter commute, clues to knowing the hearts of our spouses and children, clues to winning at work without losing our souls, clues to guide us in the spending of our days.

In decades of life and love and work I've watched for and tested the clues, rules, principles that matter and last. I've listened for insights from others, at the next desk or in the far distance of writings from thousands of miles away or thousands of years ago.

For decades the focusing (you might say obsessive) principle of my life was simply my children—providing for them, protecting them, though not always (as my wife has taught me) sharing myself fully with them. Now, as our children have grown up and out and away, and as my wife and I have re-learned (happily) how to be people and a couple, I've felt a growing urgency to write down for my children the things (or one thing) I've learned that might prevent at least some of the pain of a typical human life.

Many others have tried this through the centuries. But after spending too much time with my shoulders hunched up and asking, "Why add another effort to the pile?" I've decided the better answer is, "Why not?"

There's much I've learned in looking for an organizing principle, for the one-item checklist for how to live. Is the goal simply clear-eyed honesty in the Sisyphean effort to know others and be known ourselves? Is it the pragmatic work to standardize big chunks of our lives so we can be wildly creative in all the rest?

It is those things, for sure. But above all I now believe the core question is how much we bring ourselves to each encounter— how ready we are to exhaust our flame before it's extinguished.

Bring that energy to the pursuit of "believe, belong and matter" in your organization. You'll feel the difference.

17
MODULATE AND AMPLIFY

Humans are wonderful creatures but we create a lot of problems—for ourselves and others. A bunch of problems result when we make too much of something or not enough of something. There's the rub: it's not always clear which is which, and getting it wrong too many times with, say, a partner is a sure path to becoming either a butthead or a bore.

And there's yet another problem: If we don't have enough extremes in our life, the lack of contrast can become gray dreariness.

There's good news. Most of us lean one way or the other, either catastrophizing everything or minimizing everything. The trick is to learn which mistake you're likely to make, and then compensate for it – or at least periodically make compensation.

If you're a catastrophizer, then watch for an situation where you'd be natural to dial things way up, and play it cool—for the benefit of yourself and for anybody around you. It'll give them a break, it'll make you a little less predictable next time (healthy for everyone), and it will let you experience something different.

If you're a compulsive minimizer, pick something to dial way up—whether it's an offer for someone else or a cause for yourself. Here's where life and happiness lie—whether you're fighting to get yourself a protected hour of quiet every morning to meditate, or trying to convince your spouse that you should join the circus.

Mix things up. Don't practice just modulation or amplification; make sure you live a mix of extreme modulation and extreme amplification. Then you—and others—will notice, and get something out of them.

This alternation—I prefer not to call it "balance," which suggests a deadly mediocrity—has parallels to the ideas of two clear thinkers:

- The "barbell" strategy of Nassim Taleb, which says invest 90 percent of your resources into super-safe bets and 10 percent into crazy ones with big upsides. Translation: don't average your bets; make meaningful bets at the extremes.
- Roberto Unger's advice to "be prudent in small things the better to be reckless in big ones." Translation: take care of your basic responsibilities so you can think big and swing large.

That last angle informed a toast I made at my younger son's wedding dinner, where I advised him and his wife to do their chores, think big, and love like there's no tomorrow (because someday there won't be). He said, "Dad, that's so sad." I said, "No, I don't mean it to be sad; I mean instead that each day is a huge gift to be joyful about."

Part 3

Quick Hits and Tactical Suggestions

18
YOU NEED TO MAKE IT YOUR OWN

No communications plan begins with a truly blank page. There is always a starting point, of dream or goal, or personality or history.

This is why this book does not contain a theoretical communications plan with messaging. I can provide the likely structures, ask the questions that you need to answer, and offer scenarios and solutions for certain situations. But you need to decide what applies to you and what doesn't.

This means that I can only help you so far in this book. That's life—for both of us.

19
IT'S ABOUT THE BUSINESS

To be an effective communications pro you need to appreciate the business goals of leaders across the spectrum. And always be fostering the organization's agenda, not just feel-good stuff.

There are many reasons for this. One is that you have to remain credible to your bosses. Unless you are talking their language, of money and challenge and reality, you won't have credibility. Communications cannot be a nice-to-have, it has to be a must-do, and to establish that level of urgency you have to convince or display that you mean business.

The organization's actual agenda is a source of richness, not a bunch of constraints. Each messy, real-world problem contains opportunities for the communicator. This is because (remember) communications work isn't supposed to be a happy whitewash, but a leveraging of reality. In each of the difficult realities is actually an opportunity to make sure communications is grounded in, well, reality.

So there is a bit of a virtuous spiral here: the organization's agenda, the leadership agenda, are what you must tackle whether you like or not. On the other hand, they provide the grittiest reality that you would be willing to pay for if you had to.

20
LIKELY SCENARIOS TO PREPARE FOR

There is a handful of typical situations where there are reasonable communications responses to recommend. Here are some of them.

New leader for the organization, at any level.

This is an opportunity to introduce the leader, and more important to re-capture the spirit of what everyone is working toward. This is a great excuse to reset everything, with the leader's personality slightly in the background. It is an opportunity to dial up the heat or dial it down, to develop the gratitude or to tell folks that gratitude is going to take a backseat for a while.

Big acquisition, in either direction.

Again, like nearly every new situation, this is an opportunity to re-remind everyone why we're working so hard and what we're trying to achieve, and with the value of that will be, in hard money terms and in emotional value.

Bad result: a downturn in the core or a big account loss.

This is an opportunity for the leader to demonstrate humility, and take accountability so long as it is justified in legitimate and not a stage act. It is an opportunity for the leader to demonstrate insight, as in the analysis of what went wrong. It's an opportunity for the leader to ask for help, such as after diagnosing the problem to ask the team to work together to prevent it from ever happening again.

Great result.

An opportunity for thanks. A chance to point out the brilliance of one or more people who helped make it happen, with creativity or foresight or intelligent planning or hard work.

This is one of those opportunities and dangers at the same time, where it is tempting to thank someone for giving up their family life or harming their health in the interest of the organization, when that is not the best kind of kudos to be offering as examples. There are many other behaviors to incentivize with "thanks."

21
THE POWER OF Q&A

Include question-and-answer documents in everything you do, big and small, public and private.

It aids clarity. It helps you think in ways that normal writing or thinking don't. It invites the contrast you need for clarity—and for preparing for the unexpected.

Your Model Q&A can be about actual content or situations, demonstrating simplicity and directness, and also demonstrating the ability to surprise from time to time.

Your Q&A about employee communications itself helps you help employees: "How do I go about…?" Or "What about situations where I…?"

Your own private Q&A can be a checklist to make the best use of 5 minutes or 5 days. "What's the best use of my time at this moment?" Or "I just got handed a new assignment; where should I begin?"

Your colleague might also ask, "I have never done communications before. Where to begin?"

The Q&A is the perfect tool to model Roberto Unger's observation that "imagination does the work of crisis, without crisis."

22
MAKE THE MOST OF PROBLEMS

Take advantage of the problem situations. Make the most of even boring procedural announcements, not by adding hype but by adding depth and context and opportunistic teaching

The problem situations can offer big drama, which you can leverage by either offering equally dramatic solutions or by surprising people with boring solutions to big drama.

Even the most boring procedural announcement can be combined with reminders about strategy, or thank-you's to hero players.

One thought about hero players: these are the ongoing opportunities to salute unsung heroes as well as those who are "sung" very loudly all the time.

23
YOU DON'T HAVE TO BE AN EXTROVERT

The "anything but nonchalance" and "don't be boring" rules don't mean that only extroverts can find secular salvation. On the contrary, introverts may have an advantage in that their passion is closer to the vest, more controlled, with greater intensity stored and ready to explode.

By the textbook definitions—an extrovert is energized by being around other people, an introvert de-energized—I'm an introvert who practices being an extrovert at work.

Passion and intensity both begin as private matters, anyway. It's how you implement them that can become either public or more private.

24
SOMETIMES YOU HAVE TO SURPRISE PEOPLE

Sometimes you just have to surprise people—to get yourself, and them, out of an unhealthy rut.

They get used to hearing what they expect from you. It works the same inside ourselves, too: we each get used to thinking what we expect to think, to feeling what we expect to feel. It's a rut whether we carve it out ourselves or someone else does the carving. So we need to shake ourselves out of that rut.

How?

Look for opportunities to say or do something you believe in, but that someone else (your spouse, your boss) won't be expecting. Sometimes you can find the germ of this idea by simply paying attention to those ideas for action that are exciting at first but that you dismiss because they are beyond what you're inclined to do— and yet they'd be true for you to do. Then opt to do the thing, with vigor. These can be in any direction, up or down, in or out. It could mean paying a large compliment where it's least expected (but warranted). Or the opposite: criticizing someone more crisply than I might, or pushing a colleague harder than I would normally do.

Even great fastball pitchers need one or two other pitches to thrive.

25
REMAKE IT EVERY DAY—BECAUSE THERE'S NO OTHER OPTION

The need, and opportunity, to remake things daily is a thread that links religious faiths, professional performance, community influence, and family relationships. It's the principle that acknowledges the second law of thermodynamics—entropy.

It's a bummer, say, that my great performance on last month's project won't carry me through this year at work. Or that the big favor I did my wife yesterday won't make me more lovable tomorrow.

A bummer, yes, but only in one sense: because this law ensures fresh ideas, fresh behaviors, and a sort of collective fight against entropy.

26
HURRY—WE DON'T HAVE MUCH TIME

In 99 percent of life's projects, here's the approach that has worked best for me: Rough it out completely and quickly, then fine-tune and finish it slowly.

Do a mediocre and very fast job of the first steps. If it's the kind of project you can do in full and then improve—like a written report or proposal, or a letter of recommendation (or resignation)—then do a complete (and crappy) draft right now. Have the project ready to ship or hand off or turn away from, in its not-ready-for-prime-time form. Take the time you want to improve it.

If it's the kind of work you cannot re-do to improve (pouring the concrete for a retaining wall, or conducting bran surgery), then do the fast-crappy job virtually: think quickly through every step you'll be doing, fast.

Then think through it again, more slowly.

Then take the first steps, whatever the project and your practice dictate.

27
DON'T HURRY—WE DON'T HAVE MUCH TIME

Here's the deal. We're going to be dead a long time. Is that 3:10 bus to the mall all that important if we miss it? Or the first 10 minutes of that movie?

Which things are really worth the hurry?

So I don't exactly mean, "don't hurry." I mean, be very very selective about what we hurry about.

Even in the pursuit of "believe, belong, and matter."

28
A THEORY OF EVERYTHING?

I've decided that creating a Theory of Everything is both futile and a profound responsibility. Here's why.

Many Christmases ago, I determined to have my "final conversation" with each of my adult children—in advance of a death I hoped would follow only many years later.

I failed miserably.

My younger son was my first attempt. My guinea pig. I began. He immediately called it the "everything you've ever learned in 5 minutes" speech. And I immediately saw that my project was really designed to do more for me than for my kids. To let me relax. To feel, finally, that my job was done, so I could carry on without worrying.

The motive wasn't evil, but the execution was lacking—for him and for me.

I went back to the drawing board.

In the time since I've thought about this a lot. My intent. My goal. The folly of trying to capture all the important things. And the responsibility of trying anyway.

We'll to never get fully to "believe, belong, and matter." But most of the gain is in the quest to get there.

29
THE POWER OF SIMPLE CLARITY

Question: How clear can you get—and how fast?

In communications, isn't that what makes the difference between a small quick win of a moment, and just another moment lost to time?

Listen. Why don't we humans learn from generation to generation, through the blood? Isn't the process of showing the next generation how to do something the crudest thing you've ever seen? It's like deciding to build a car with a hand crank ignition instead of using the invented internal ignition.

Gaining clarity for myself is one thing. Teaching others to gain clarity for themselves is another. Yet the most effective, the greatest achievement, would be a self-sustaining clarity—one that continued on, scalable, not requiring the body shop of parents and managers and mentors to hand it down in a clumsy, inelegant one-on-one training series.

Sustainable clarity is clarity that feeds on itself. That draws on this moment's clarity to inform and infuse the next moment's clarity—insight for the generations. Sustainable insights.

David Deutsch says that most ideas aren't replicable. My challenge is to create an idea, a theory of organizational communication, that does spread, like the wildfire or a virus or clichés themselves or good manners, fast and smooth. Why? Because of its utility and its beauty, its pragmatism and its elegance.

But it can't be created safely. It has to be risky, it has to be bold enough to risk ridicule.

So, what have I learned in four decades of communications work and thoughtful attention that could change others' thinking and their lives? It's this: When we're thinking or talking or writing, we must express our ideas as simply, as sharply, as possible if we're to have any hope of (a) truly knowing what we're actually thinking and (b) truly sharing it with another human.

Only when we can express something with simple nouns and verbs can we test it to see if we're full of hot air. This is hard, because being full of hot air is embarrassing (even if it's a secret). So it's tempting to keep things foggy, because then we never risk that shame.

Instead, let's teach those we care about—from toddlers in pre-K to leaders in board rooms—that it's better to feel the shame of baloney and then move on to the pride of clear progress.

30
AVOIDING HOLLOW-SOUNDING INSPIRATION

A book with a theme of "believe, belong, matter" can easily slip into the language of inspirational posters with beautifully lighted photographs that suggest clarity and altitude. I hope to do better for you.

I believe communications can help an organization and its people achieve situations or qualities that feel as good as those beautifully lighted photographs. But the path there is seldom beautiful. It's not necessarily ugly, but it is filled with tasks from boring to exciting. And plenty of procedural work to make sure that people know how to fill out their tax forms and, if you're lucky enough to have a gym, people know how to get lockers were clean towels.

Baseline work is necessary so that people have the energy and attention to absorb the wondrous matters.

The communicator has a special opportunity: she is dedicated to communications and does not have to directly worry about profit. But at the same time she (if she is lucky and has earned a seat at the table) has a view toward everything that is going on and can put it in terms of communications opportunities and challenges, for leaders to leverage or for the unsigned communications vehicles to make the most of.

31
SURPRISING ROLE MODELS

What can we learn from Joan Rivers?

The Joan Rivers archives—the file cabinets and card boxes—teach us how painstaking and detail-oriented the otherwise smooth and seamless presentation of comedy is and must be.

It wasn't just compulsion that had Joan keeping card-catalog shelves full of jokes. It was a recognition, conscious or unconscious, that each of those jokes is fleeting unless captured. I suspect there was also an ability to build on things that were captured.

My two other favorite examples of unlikely role models, of the blend of creativity plus discipline, are Clint Eastwood and Saul Bellow. Each of them is well known for being buttoned up about their process, which both fuels and frees creativity and gets out of its way to prevent distraction and noise.

In Eastwood's case, it was about budget and schedule. In Bellow's case it was about the daily grind of additive progress.

32
ASK FOR HELP FROM ONE PERSON AT A TIME

If you need help, write an email to *one* person at a time, not more.

How do you build responsibility with *all* employees? Find a way to make each individual employee feel like an owner—feel like the company's entire success depends on them alone.

They *matter*.

33
FOCUS AND STAMINA

Stamina and discipline are critical to KEEP messaging what you've started. And they're hard.

That was the lesson I learned after a big "Wired for Management" event that Intel held at Madison Square Garden in the mid-90s. The event had called for an entirely new messaging architecture. We were proud of it, our stakeholders loved it, and we felt great.

During one review session right before the event, there was a bullet on a slide that talked about the sequences of messaging evolution for the next one month, six months, one year, two years. My boss, the senior executive of PR, chuckled. He said something like, "it's pretty to think so."

He was right of course. Messaging discipline started to erode shortly after the very successful event. How does this happen? How do teeth brushing and push-up disciplines erode?

How to compensate for this? Force of will does not work. Setting up incentives and routines is the only way to proceed. What your version of incentives and routines are almost doesn't matter, so long as you try something. Contests for communications activities that are closest to the message house? Publishing of highlights or shame-lights on the internal intranet?

One good approach is to have a dashboard of messaging compliance. Report on it weekly or monthly.

Try something. Fight inertia—and overconfidence.

34
TRY GRATITUDE

Humans love to be thanked for their efforts. Employees are humans. Employees would appreciate feeling gratitude from their leaders.

Gratitude is one of my most powerful emotions. For example, the profound feelings of gratitude I have had when a receptionist at the doctor's office solves a problem or the other night when the pharmacist helped me get a late-night prescription.

They gave me more help than they needed to provide.

What is the communications implication for this emotion? In a big way it's about being easy to do business with and about delivering on your promises.

For us as communicators, this dynamic applies in all of our relationships, both strategic and transactional. It applies to your relationship with the executives of your organization.

It applies to the relationship that employees perceive with the organization itself. Making tax forms easy. Making equipment easy to get.

And it goes all the way to the clarity and honesty of communications. Make things easy to understand. Don't make people work harder than they need to.

The more energy you conserve, the more is available, by all parties, to trust more and to aim higher.

35
HOW BIG (AND WHERE) DOES YOUR TEAM NEED TO BE?

How big does your internal communications team need to be, how should it be structured, and where should it be located in the organization?

The answer, of course, is it depends.

You can think about having the size of your internal communications team be flexible and fungible, by having a small core group of constant professionals and adding to it an orbit of part-time dedicated souls.

You can scale the size and texture of your team to the situation. You may have a large change effort underway, requiring a bigger team. Or you may be operating with a trusted and tested message house and a broad network of implicit volunteers, allowing you to have a very very small team alone.

More important to me than size is the *organizational location* of the internal communications team. I used to be agnostic about this, feeling that the internal communications team could be a part of marketing, or PR, and be equally effective as it would be in human resources. The notion behind that agnosticism is that you get the benefit of being inside one particular team, and then you compensate by partnering with others not in your immediate organization.

For example, since an internal communications team needs to be well-connected with employees and their health, and well-connected with the business and its market mission, I used to think the internal communications team could be in marketing, have the benefit of a direct connection to the business, and then partner compulsively with human resources to add that connection to employees.

I no longer an agnostic. I believe that internal communications will be strongest when it is within human resources, absorbing and living with all of the trials and tribulations of employee talent, strength, and struggles.

Behind my change of mind is the recognition that it is easier to partner on the shared intellectual values and harder to grasp those emotions long-distance. So I would rather the (forgive the stereotype) "heart based" elements of employee life be directly connected to internal communications. Thus, reside in human resources.

36
OPERATING AT TWO SPEEDS

The best communications teams can operate at two levels in two speeds: long and detailed and comprehensive, and quick and dirty and messy. With equal comfort and effectiveness.

This ambidextrous capability is important not only because there are situations and timings that will require both. But it is also the case that when you can do either mode, you feel safer to be operating in either mode.

When you're doing a long and complex strategy that requires lots of iteration and lots of review, it is good to know that at a moment's notice you can shift it down and dirty from urgency happens.

Conversely, when you're doing down-and-dirty it is comforting to know that you're not doing this because it is all you can do, but because it is what you choose to do for this situation.

This reminds me of the need, in any big project, to be "ready to get it out the door." Even in a long and complex, many iteration, project, I like to have a dirty version cooked and baked at the beginning, so that if circumstance (or an executive boss) dictated that the time was up, we could simply reach into the drawer (figuratively) and hand over the "finished" project.

37
PRETEND IT ALL DEPENDS ON YOU

As internal communications folks we need to embrace the conceit the responsibility that everything depends on us. That lets us—pushes us—to discover and uncover everything or as much of everything that could be discovered.

Then we have the mixed blessing of discovering the realities of our limits, the limits of our power, the recognition that we can't do it all ourselves. And then the realization that that's a good thing (we have one clear voice) and a happy thing because we have all the other voices and skills and modes of others to help us.

As communication advisers, we need to be ready always to give our leaders a recommendation, no matter how imperfect.

It might just depend on us.

38
BE READY TO RENT EXPERTISE

You don't need to have every talent on your team. Just know where to find the expert guides or the support crews when you need them, in such areas as:

- Presentations
- Writing of all flavors
- Press training (not for hiding but careful direct clarity)
- Graphics
- Events

39
GETTING UNSTUCK

One of the obstacles to clarity is "stuckness."

One of the ways we get stuck is by making too much of a situation or a decision—as if our lives and the judgment of the ages about our value will depend on what I do or accomplish here.

It's helpful to me to steal, at such moments, the notion of "nothing special" from the Zen author Charlotte Joko Beck. Who will know in a hundred years or maybe a hundred minutes what transpired here? Perhaps it's not quite as consequential as we feared.

Yet does it warrant our good-faith effort? What if it's our last action before the bus hits us? OK, 60 seconds of clarity will be good here.

40
SPEED WRITING AND SPEED THINKING

A familiar trick to remove writer's block is to force yourself to write continuously for 5 or 10 or 30 minutes, without pause and sometimes without even lifting your pen from the page.

What does this have to teach us about clarity?

Try it. It's interesting sometimes how gems of insight emerge, as if you were panning for gold and, by increasing the flow for those 30 minutes, increasing the amount of ore you are processing.

You can try this with or without a keyboard or a pen: do some "speed thinking" to spike the mount of ore you're mining for some precious-metal clarity.

41
ORAL TRADITION

In teaching writing I've sometimes invited students to "say out loud" the first draft of their work when they can't get traction in written form.

This works in two important ways.

One, it unsticks many a block. After all, who won't speak to their friend standing nearby?

Two, it often de-formalizes our language and thus clarifies things.

It's one of the simplest tricks to break through to clarity—and one of the hardest to get ourselves to do.

Just say it out loud.

Whatever we're thinking, trying to think, planning or trying to plan, we can get it clear to ourselves often by just voicing it out loud.

This trick can get us ready for a speech, it can dislodge a tough written passage, and it can bring to the front of mind some tough (or joyful) thoughts that are lurking or stuck in the back of mind.

42
IMITATE THE GREATS
(BY NOT IMITATING THEM)

Clichés are one of the worst viruses to infect our thinking and exhaust our clarity.

The great writers, speakers and thinkers have this in common: they look for the fresh way to express themselves, and don't rely on tired phrases that are so familiar they go right past our eyes and ears like the freeway noise we ignore.

Someone once said, "If it rolls off your tongue, it's a cliché."

The word "cliché" comes from printing, where a "cliché" was a plate of a certain design that you imprinted over and over again into paper.

The power of fresh expressions and fresh ideas isn't about esthetics or art: it's about not relaxing into a cookie-cutter approach of sameness that relieves us of the duty to ask ourselves, "what exactly am I thinking or feeling or meaning right now?"

No employee gets to "believe, belong, and matter" by hearing the same things in the same ways that she's heard for ages.

43
CHESS MASTER

What amazed me most about Bobby Fisher and Boris Spassky wasn't their sheer brilliance but their discipline—thinking through the implications of the next 10 or 100 possible moves.

Any kind of planning helps our clarity in two important ways.

One, it makes our intentions clear (to ourselves and our family/partner/friends/colleagues/bystanders), not only for our next step but the ones after it.

Two, it helps us decide whether the first step is the right one, by testing out mentally the ramifications of that first step.

One military general once said that long-term strategy documents were worthless, but the *process of thinking through the strategy* was priceless.

44
EDITOR IN CHIEF

Getting to clarity is an iterative process.

The clear idea, intention, plan, or expression seldom emerges sharp. Instead, the owner who cares about it makes it become what it can become, through tuning, sanding, practicing.

It helps to think of ourselves as editors rather than writers. That does mean we need to draft continually, so that we'll have ideas and intentions to edit into clarity.

45
WITHOUT DISCIPLINE, WE GOT NOTHING

Beautiful messaging does nothing if it's not delivered.

And in an organization, it's not "delivered" unless it's delivered on time, in the right places, with the right tone, countless times, by the right mix of speakers and other message-carriers.

That takes careful planning, disciplined execution, and stamina.

46
AUGUSTINE AND DARWIN

One of the paradoxical obstacles to communications clarity is the pursuit of perfection.

Even that phrase, "the pursuit of perfection," feels tired to me.

I've never successfully diagrammed the clichéd expression, "The perfect is the enemy of the good," because I've never quite been sure how the nouns and verbs and modifiers are supposed to be read there. But the core idea I agree with, because I've suffered with it in two ways, one worthy of compassion and one worthy of ridicule.

First, the sense that "this must be perfect" may be a human flaw but it certainly is a Catholic one, and I'm genetically catholic. Relax, I tell myself and my friends.

Second, the sense that "I can make this perfect if I just have time or space or [fill in the blank]" is an arrogant view that (a) blows my talents way out of proportion and (b) lets me postpone actually doing something while I wait for that perfect moment. Baloney.

So here I get both comfort and energy from St. Augustine and from the insights of Charles Darwin.

Augustine's reluctant transformation, as the story goes—"God give me chastity, but not yet"—tells me that my imperfections and hesitance to change them have me in good company.

Darwin's realization that living things evolve in a grand and complex game of test-and-see gives me some comfort about a life of tinkering.

And these are reminders that the best people aren't the ones who could envision the future and get there without bruises, but rather those who had strong intentions, at varying levels of clarity, and kept moving forward to test and tune and refine them—ever towards clarity, and then a new clarity.

Ever towards "believe, belong and matter."

47
NOT (JUST) VISION

People who achieve great things are often lionized as having great visions—a view of the future that they clearly perceived and then worked to realize.

Rubbish. In my experience such people have three things:

- an idea
- an extreme ability to focus with discipline
- a willingness to be radical in their behavior or their reputation on the way to getting there

I'm not diminishing the accomplishment of such folks. On the contrary, I'm more impressed all the time by their accomplishments—because I increasingly recognize that they were not super-humans but have DNA that's 99.99 percent like you and me. That makes their achievements all the more impressive.

In the books *The Origin of Wealth* and *The Black Swan*, the authors independently offer two theses that provide an interesting perspective on extreme achievements if you read them right.

The Black Swan shows (among other points) how we use a logical fallacy called confirmation bias to create narratives of highly successful people that make the progress seem logical and orderly (visionary) when in fact it is an after-the-fact line connecting events that each had a small chance of occurring. We hear a linear and logical story when there was no such order or predictability.

In *The Origin of Wealth* Eric Beinhocker gives a powerful telling of how many steps go into manifesting the global economy each day—buying and selling and shipping and staging and deciding—so many of them driven not by the so-called "perfect rationality" of economic man but instead by a trillion human judgments or non-judgments, each dependent on the judgments that came before and each influencing those to follow.

So what?

I'm not recommending a nihilist view that "all is random, so give it up."

Rather I'm suggesting that readiness and flexibility are everything. That an ability to respond to changing circumstances is as valuable as learning algebra and chemistry, and that learning a bit of algebra and chemistry and English grammar are essential for having the foundation of readiness that we all need to thrive.

I'm suggesting that planning carefully is more, not less, important in this world as the complexity and interdependency go up, because you need to remove the unknowns you can in order to leave intellectual and spiritual energy for the increasing unknowns about to be hurled your way each day.

48
LEANING INTO PUNCHES

"Lean into a punch" is good advice with multiple meanings.

There's the literal punch, the literal lean, and the defiant message best captured in the movie Raging Bull ("you never got me down, Ray").

There's the lesson that fast and clear pain is better than slow, drawn-out and foggy pain.

And then there's the intelligence-gathering and insight-seeking strategy: how much can I learn from this punch, whether from a person or circumstance, that might either teach me something for later or give me a view to making this crummy situation turn out to my advantage?

When the mythical IBM salesman responds to the scathing complaint by saying, "Tell me more," he doesn't stop there. He *listens*.

How much can I learn from this punch?

What does this punch tell me about the organizational obstacles to "believe, belong and matter"? Where should I lean in and listen next?

49
CHANGING THE GAME – OR CONVERSATION

Once I was on was asked to talk to a small group about how to handle getting knocked down or shot down by a customer or client, and how to recover and thrive. I drew a diagram on a flip chart and asked my audience to think about the "dials" they could turn to change the game, or at least change the situation.

The gist is that you can mentally review (a) what would help you most in the situation, (b) what would repair or recover or change the tone, and (c) what could give you some more power or leverage.

In the diagram, each line is a "dial" and the two extremes at each end of the line give you a sense of what you can dial up or down. One is the range from confidence to humility; one is a range from predictability to surprise; and one is the range from push (speaking or offering) to pull (asking or listening).

These are three spectra you can mentally review and select from. For example, if your gut tells you that you've been too predictable, you can seek a way to surprise (with action or tone, or even one of the other vectors). If the other person is feeling too unsettled from too many surprises, then seeking a way to deliver predictability in a concrete, palpable way could be a solution. You get the idea.

Similarly if a setting or a person has had too much cockiness or humility from you, change the game. If you've been on the receiving end too much (of input or advice or outbursts), it's time

123

to push back or simply push your own advice onto the other person or the situation, and vice versa.

There's no rocket science here, but the power is in having these notions available to readily review in your mind, and then the action can be a tool that's ready to use.

50
BLOWHARDS

In our communications work, it's hard to know sometimes who is a blowhard and who isn't. There are two important parts of this. One is being able to recognize a blowhard, and getting better over time at it (faster and better identification, etc.). The other part, though, is simply being willing to declare someone a blowhard (even if only privately).

I've wasted a lot of time in my life by not being willing to declare someone such (even to myself). I recommend you adopt a willingness to do so when needed. You'll still waste time sometimes by getting it wrong, but at least you don't guarantee the time loss by refusing to judge.

You'll get the judging wrong sometimes about who's a blowhard, who's full of baloney, who just looks like a blowhard. You can get confused between someone who uses aphorisms and aspirational sayings to achieve better performance, and who uses them to simply have a refrain to sing to self-amuse or make excuses without any notion of context.

Take, for example, those cheerleading quotations that many people put at the bottom of their signature on emails. I hate those little quotations; I don't want to BE those sayings, and I don't need to brand myself with the stuff. At play here is my own reverse-arrogance, my own reverse-snobbery, for sure. But I still hate those little sayings, unequivocally.

Now, I once had a colleague at work who used this kind of quotation at the end of her emails, and this colleague is a stand-up person whom I admired. Another colleague used one, and I could just hear it (painfully for me) being spoken in his voice as he would rant about not enough freedom and creativity being fostered in our work.

These are often the same kinds of folks who complain that they are not given enough running room to be creative—who ask for the "opportunity to be strategic"—and don't take responsibility to not just wait for an invitation but instead look for ways to inject creativity into anything they are doing, whether self-chosen or dictated.

So you can't judge a person JUST on one of these markers, though they do help sometimes.

(By the way, I believe that you can inject creativity and innovation into ANY action or situation if you can figure it out. The situation itself is never an absolute limiter.)

51
THE POWER OF 'NEXT'

Two authors who could not be more different—Roberto Unger and David Allen—share an appreciation of "next." And "next" is a powerful tool for communicators.

In ways sacred and profane, these authors focus on the importance and power of "the next thing." Unger tells us that a central question thru our lives should be, "what should we do next?" to move our personal and social existence forward. He adds that in this way, living for the future makes sense, because that's how we envision the better case, through imagination, that we want to achieve—and we achieve it by taking action, by experimenting, by being "prudent in small things so that we may be reckless in big things."

In *The Self-Awakened*, Unger writes: "What allows us to ask at every turn the question—what should we do next?—is the marriage of the imagination with an existential attitude: a hopeful and patient availability to novelty and to experience."

David Allen suggests that the path to "stress-free productivity" is to capture and understand our commitments and goals and then to decide and declare the "next actions"—the concrete next steps to move forward toward the desired outcome.

"The big key is 'next action,'" Allen writes in *Getting Things Done*. "What's the very next physical, visible activity, and where does it happen?"

No question packs more profound and pragmatic power than "what's next?"

52
LISTEN

Listening may be the single most powerful communications tool—for changing lives or changing views. For getting to "believe, belong and matter."

Listen. What do you hear? Uncertainty? Focus? Are you hearing the thoughts flow between you and the person you're hearing?

There are few limits to what you can learn by listening.

So what?

It's the single most neglected skill in the human toolbox. So many of our emotions militate against it. We want to correct what we are hearing. We wish to be seen differently. We want not to hear what our speaker is about to say.

In that broad human neglect lies a big advantage. You can distinguish yourself from ordinary folks by listening. And listening gives you the added advantage of knowing more, understanding more. This differentiates you further.

Where to start? Ask questions.

And then: Listen.

Listen closely to what your teammates, partners, stakeholders, bosses and employees are saying. You'll learn a lot—which will help you understand, plan, and act.

Listen not only to their words, but also for what they're trying to say. Ask good questions. That'll help you understand even better—and maybe help them understand better, too.

By listening, you'll also help others know they're being heard. That pays off in so many ways for everyone. Then they'll tell you more. That'll pay off some more, for everyone. And, and, and....

Leaders who don't interrupt their staff members (or other employees in open forums) not only build trust and community, but learn things they wouldn't get to otherwise.

Listen to your own voice, too. It's as important an input as others'. Ask yourself good questions—to help you understand even better, plan better, take better action, or know when not to act.

53
NOUNS, VERBS AND RUBBISH

If we can learn to write clearly, we can think clearly, and live clearly.

It's simply about being willing to write what you think, without fog, stripping away the wrappings and trappings that let us think the thought is good because its flaws are unclear.

It's the same with clarity about our life decisions: we are afraid to look at them bare and stripped of artifice, because then it's impossible to avoid judging them honestly, and often harshly.

So be it with our writing, whether we're writing about a task or a dream. Let it be clearly what it is, with simple nouns and verbs offering the declarative statement for all to judge, and the judgment for all to value.

Let it be with our leadership and communications work toward "believe, belong and matter."

And let then the task or dream stand for what it has to, without fog to distract or, worse, to numb.

54
WRITING TO LIVE

Writing with clarity is a useful metaphor for living with clarity. It's also a good test. If you can't write down your plans and your after-action summaries in simple sentences with nouns, verbs and objects, then you're not going to be thinking clearly enough about your life to get the important stuff right.

Try this:

1. Write the last chapter. Know how you want things to end—and plan carefully for both that ending and the other, worst-case, scenario you fear. Plan for both. Rehearse them mentally so you can envision and work toward the best one, and to exorcize the power from the worst.

2. Examine (or if you're a grammarian, diagram) the one-sentence opening summary of what you want to accomplish. Look at the verbs. Are they the strongest ones you can find? Or do they lean toward the passive voice? In life, as in writing, passive voice is deadly—it has no place in an opening or a closing line, because it leaves too much to chance.

3. Vary the cadence. A narrative with only one sentence rhythm and one length can lose the reader. A life with only one theme probably means someone is losing out—either your loved ones or you. A single routine is a symptom you should check out. Just as in writing, it may be exactly the result you want, but you should ask and answer the

question, "Is it really the desired result?" You don't want to get there accidentally.

4. Make the transitions work for you. In a narrative the most powerful messages come from the changes in characters. In life and work the times of change are the opportunities for power, for a risk you might not have taken otherwise, for a view that had to be forced on you. Watch for these changes and leverage them. If they don't emerge, then create them.

5. Draft constantly and edit freely. The payoffs are large. Getting a "draft 0" down on paper gets you started, and starting is most of everything. Some of us are better editors—of words, of ideas, of life plans—than we are writers and creators. Many great writers have said they were really just very good editors, but they made sure they created the "crappy little ideas" for starters. It applies to the first draft of your communications plan, it applies to your plan for life, and it applies to actions themselves. "First draft" can mean first date, first day on the job, first music lesson, or simply showing up at the soup kitchen without an appointment. It doesn't have to be perfect, or even workable; it just has to exist for starters.

55
CREDIT: THE UNLIMITED RENEWABLE RESOURCE

It's always strikes me as foolish when someone is stingy with credit, as in acknowledging the contribution others make toward a good outcome. (I'm not free of blame here.)

Perhaps most common in the workplace, this ungenerosity can happen anywhere. This "credit" is different from praise and recognition, which are related and important forces. I'm talking about the basic foundational action of giving someone credit due for the work they've done.

This kind of credit is one of the few unlimited renewable resources. And in the workplace it's perhaps the most foolishly underused resource. It's one of the most powerful tools toward the "matter" part of "believe, belong and matter."

Of course, it must be truly and honestly earned before it can be of any worth. But there's plenty of it to go around. It builds strength and confidence when offered.

When given, especially in the sometimes stingy environments that personal competitiveness engenders, it's a powerful force for progress.

We should share credit more. It multiplies.

56
HEROISM IN OUR ORGANIZATION

In our cynical times the notion of heroism is often sneered at as inflated and unmodern. But a much longer tradition underscores its power, usefulness and guidance.

When we feel a small spark of large possibility, we're in touch with the heroic in ourselves. When we're struggling to be more human and less reptilian, we're in touch with the heroic. It's the aim-very-high prescription for achieving (or being) something acceptable.

It can help fuel the "believe" part of our organizational framework.

May Sarton captured this: "One must think like a hero to behave like a merely decent human being."

57
STRUGGLE

Communications work is hard. It can feel like the goals are aspirational and thus never reachable. We have many masters. We pursue "believe, belong, and matter" and never are sure how we're doing.

Do not let this book make you feel guilty if you're sad, tired, stuck, scared, dejected, exhausted or feeling jaded—sometimes or much of the time.

Humans are vulnerable in the best of times. And life brings us much more than just the best of times.

You lose your job. Your child becomes seriously ill. Fire or flood destroys your home and all you own. Mental illness darkens your days and saps your will to struggle on.

The company has a product flaw that threatens its existence. There's an economic downturn.

"Struggle on" is sometimes the only thing you can do. "Struggle on" may be the most heroic thing you ever do.

In our own lives and in the life of our organization, these and countless other struggles are real, the challenges seemingly (sometimes truly) insurmountable. They can't be erased by a happy outlook or by willing yourself to apply the "passion and commitment" that my "believe, belong, matter" framework depends upon.

Happy messaging won't do it, either.

If you're in these holes, it doesn't mean you're failing, or that you're just not adopting the right point of view. "Nonchalance" is not your problem; it's a high-class problem that you wish was yours.

But in your struggle to help employees believe, to care for your family, to get a job, to fight through whatever darkness you face, remember that *everything follows action*—the next opportunity, the help from a surprising source, even more motivation and energy to take the next step in the struggle, no matter how small that step might be.

Struggling onward is anything but nonchalance.

It gets easier.

For most of us, the struggle does, in fact, get easier. The big decisions are still intense. A long day is still long. But for every hour (or hundred hours) of experience, you get learning memories that you instinctively apply in the future. For every decision (or hundreds of decisions) you have a bigger database of inputs and outcomes to draw upon.

Of course, a big workload is still a big workload. But that aggregating knowledge is a powerful force for both effectiveness and efficiency. Most valuable, it fuels a growing instinct for the boundaries you can draw, when you "know" that more analysis won't improve the outcome, and when you "know" you can or should turn it all off.

But you have to remind yourself of these gains, and pay active attention to them, because our normal human brains don't fully appreciate them.

58
EMPATHY FOR LEADERS

Have sympathy and empathy for those executives and other leaders who fall short of true leadership and honest communications. Because those things are very hard.

And it is difficult in surprising ways to maintain the focus and to do the right things.

How can you help?

59
PLANS

When you first realize that
The rules apply to you, too,
You know the signs have been
Appearing—subtly, insidiously—
Right here but out of view.

"Who knew?" you'd like to ask,
But there's no refuge there.
Ignorance is no defense, and even
If it were, there's no reprieve from
The deluge that follows the moist air.

No philosophy keeps the landlord
From the gate, no force of will
Expands tonight's cheated sleep
Into restful strength by morning.
Hope alone makes no torrent still.

Let me be explicit: The
Homework not home-worked tonight
Must yet inform this year's result.
A leap not made, a love not met,
Will tune the fading of the light.

Nothing special is the verdict
We receive from biology and physics.
In simple truck in base bazaars
Or lofty dreams felt only once, the

Rules hold sway, in cells and ticks.

The lost-wrench hunt steals time.
What distracted soul can life enthrall?
No earnestness can lift the biscuit dough
That's absent baking powder un-re-stocked.
A fool earns what he gets. That's all.

But give hope its due respect—
Rise at dawn to halt the tide's ascent,
Or fight sleep long past midnight to take
The thousand steps to joy—then hope
Makes real the impossible event.

About the Author

Michael Green is a communications professional whose four decades of work have included all forms of business communications: marketing and advertising, media and analyst relations, executive communications and employee communications. He and his wife live in Portland, Oregon.

www.ingramcontent.com/pod-product-compliance
Lightning Source LLC
Chambersburg PA
CBHW020156200326
41521CB00006B/387